The Magic of
Disneyland®
and
Walt Disney World®

By
VALERIE CHILDS

Designed and Produced by
TED SMART and DAVID GIBBON

WINDWARD

IT would be impossible to write about the magical realms of DISNEYLAND and WALT DISNEY WORLD without mentioning something of the life and work of their ingenious and enterprising creator. Born in Chicago in 1901, Walter Elias Disney was the fourth son of a building contractor, who when young Walt was only five years old, moved his family to a farm outside Marceline, Missouri. Walt's two elder brothers, Herbert and Raymond, both in their teens and preferring city life, returned to Chicago but Walt and his other brother Roy, with whom he was to develop a particularly close relationship, remained to help their parents on the farm. It was a hard life but one which Walt later remembered with affection for it was here that he first developed his interest in drawing.

The Disney family's attempts at farming were unsuccessful and in 1910 they sold the farm and moved to Kansas City where Elias, Walt's father, bought a newspaper delivery business. Once again the boys were expected to help, this time by getting up in the early hours of the morning to meet the *Kansas City Star* trucks but Walt was becoming increasingly interested in art and in a rare gesture of indulgence his father allowed him to join Saturday classes at the Kansas City Art Institute.

The family was soon on the move again however, for Elias had purchased a share in a small factory in Chicago, and there Walt received further art instruction from a newspaper cartoonist, Leroy Gossett. In 1917, brother Roy joined the Navy and Walt too had dreams of enlisting but he was still under age. At sixteen, he did however, manage to become a Red Cross driver attached to a military canteen in Neufchâteau, France where, to earn himself a few extra francs, he became the unit's unofficial artist.

Disney returned to Kansas City in 1919 and found work in a local studio. There he befriended Ubbe ('Ub') Iwerks, a young man of Dutch descent and an exceptionally talented draughtsman who was to become the most important associate of his early career. It was together with Iwerks that Disney later joined the Kansas City Slide Company, subsequently known as the Kansas City Film Ad, a company which made commercials for display in local movie theaters. Kansas City Film Ad was in fact producing crude animated films, and it provided Disney with the experience and capital to set up on his own under the title of 'Laugh-o-Grams'. Walt was ambitious

and immediately started work on a series of updated fairy tales: 'Cinderella', 'The Four Musicians of Bremen', 'Goldie Locks and the Three Bears', 'Jack and the Beanstalk', 'Little Red Riding Hood' and 'Puss in Boots'. All were expertly made but unfortunately did not sell. Disney tried to salvage the venture by making a movie in which a human heroine could cavort with cartoon characters, 'Alice's Wonderland' but he was nevertheless forced to close his studio.

Undeterred, Walt took a train to Los Angeles and moved in with his Uncle Robert. The year was 1923 and part of it he spent in his uncle's garage, building a stand for his newly acquired animation camera. Gradually Walt employed new staff, including an Idaho girl, Lillian Bounds, who two years later became his wife. Then, in 1928 Mickey Mouse, probably the most famous and best loved cartoon character was 'born'. Iwerks, by this time the finest animator of his day, was undoubtedly responsible for Mickey's physical characteristics, Walt for his personality; and so Walt and Roy, who had joined him, began work on the very first Mickey Mouse Cartoons. Disney wanted Mickey to have real impact and recognized that the future lay with sound... in the synchronization of music, effects and action. After endless experimentation 'Steamboat Willie' was launched. From his debut, Mickey contained a little germ of real personality, to which Disney himself added an ideal squeaky falsetto (a role he continued to fill for twenty years) and so began a series of cartoons starring the creature of mythic stature, who still delights the world.

With Mickey Mouse firmly established, Walt channelled his energies into the making of a feature length animated film that would provide the opportunity to expand both the characters and the plot and the story he chose was 'Snow White and the Seven Dwarfs'. It took three years to complete this, one of the most successful of Disney's films, but after a struggle against apparently insurmountable difficulties, both technical and financial, the Hollywood premiere was held before an audience of celebrities in 1937 and was given a rapturous reception.

Disney's fame spread and he went on to produce nature films like the 'Living Desert', films with human casts such as 'Mary Poppins', '20,000 Leagues Under the Sea', 'Pollyanna' and 'The Love Bug', films with the haunting musical scores of for example 'Pinocchio' and above all, films which like 'Dumbo', 'Bambi', 'Jungle Book' and innumerable others gave to the world a myriad of his enchanting and unforgettable characters.

Left: The figure who features so prominently in both DISNEYLAND and WALT DISNEY WORLD... the lovable Mickey Mouse.

Walt Disney was not, however, content merely to make films. His incomparable powers of imagination and foresight, together with his ability to think on a large scale, gave birth to the Magic Kingdoms of DISNEYLAND and WALT DISNEY WORLD, in which the lovable characters that had made his films so popular play a vital role. DISNEYLAND was the first park to be built and its impact was enormous. Although on a much smaller scale than the WALT DISNEY WORLD that was to follow, DISNEY-LAND was a truly remarkable achievement.

At the dedication ceremony on July 17th 1955, before a glittering array of personalities and public figures, Walt Disney gave voice to the intention that lay behind his creation: 'I don't want the public to see the world they live in while they're in the park, I want them to feel they are in another world.' His inaugural speech continued with the words: "Welcome. DISNEYLAND is your land. Here age relives fond memories of the past…and youth may savor the challenge and promise of the future. DISNEYLAND is dedicated to the ideals, the dreams and the hard facts that have created America…with the hope that it will be a source of joy and inspiration to the world." DISNEYLAND was in fact the fulfilment of Disney's own dream, a dream first inspired by the amusement parks and playgrounds to which he had taken his young daughters and which he had found dull and uninteresting. He had first considered building a "magical little park" on two acres of land next to his Burbank Studio, equipped with pony rides, singing waterfalls, a train and of course, with statues of Disney characters. Pressure of work and the intervention of the Second World War postponed the scheme however, until in the 1950s a far more ambitious plan requiring more land was devised. Walt sent a team of employees into the rapidly developing Orange County and they secured a 160 acre orange grove, conveniently situated next to the modern Santa Ana Freeway.

Unfortunately the ever-cautious world of financiers was reluctant to support the project and, as *Newsweek* magazine reported some years later: "To build DISNEYLAND, Walt and his brother Roy Disney borrowed to the corporate hilt and then Walt sold his vacation home at a loss and borrowed against his personal life insurance policies." Other amusement park owners scorned Walt's idea, believing that without ferris wheels and other traditional attractions, the venture was doomed. However, the timely signing of a seven year contract with the American Broadcasting Company for a weekly one hour television show paved the way for the suc-

cess of DISNEYLAND. Disney recognized in television a means of introducing his 'dream' into the homes of millions of Americans. He named the show, which first appeared in the fall of 1954, 'Disneyland' and with its immediate popularity came the financial means to build his theme park.

The land in Orange County was "all flat…no rivers, no mountains, no castle or rocket ships… just orange groves and a few acres of walnut trees" but all this was to change. Disney formed the W.E.D. (Walter Elias Disney) Enterprises, an 'imagineering' team of experts in the field of sculpture, architecture, engineering and special effects to work out the details of design and construction. The aim was to create a series of stories, each represented as a sequence of events, through which visitors would be led on a route skilfully designed so that no scene could be missed. They would experience the adventures not so much as spectators but rather as 'participants'. Originally there were five distinct themed areas, beginning with Main Street, representing small town America at the turn of the century 1890–1910. Here charming horse-drawn trolleys, horseless carriages or "putt-putts" and double-decked buses make regular journeys along Main Street, evoking memories of a more leisurely era. The street itself is lined with a variety of charming old shops and cafés including a Penny Arcade, an Ice Cream Parlor and an Emporium. The Main Street Opera House features such fascinating entertainment as "Great Moments with Mr. Lincoln," an Audio-Animatronics salute to America's 16th president and a presentation of the Walt Disney Story. Of the 100,000 light bulbs used in DISNEYLAND 11,000 outline the buildings on Main Street and when the bulbs have exhausted 80% of their life expectancy, they are replaced so that the light never fades.

The other 'lands' fan out from Main Street. In Adventureland, based on the True-Life Adventure films the visitor is transported into the steaming jungles of Africa and Asia. Canopied launches journey down alligator and hippopotamus infested rivers while cannibals and wild animals threaten from the undergrowth of the river banks. Frontierland recalls the dangerous but exciting pioneer days, when courageous men and their families crossed the continent in the face of hostile Indians and harsh weather conditions. The Davy Crockett Arcade, the Frontier Shooting Gallery (repainted each day before the park opens) and the

Scenes from Walt Disney's films *right* 'bring to life' magical moments from 'Snow White', 'Bambi', 'Cinderella', 'Peter Pan', 'Alice In Wonderland' and 'Winnie the Pooh'.

Rivers of America which surround Tom Sawyer Island are just a few of the special attractions which can be viewed from the waters of the Rivers of America in rafts, canoes, keel boats or the Mark Twain paddlewheel steamboat, or from the decks of the *Columbia*, an authentic replica of the first American ship to sail round the world in 1790.

In Fantasyland, Walt Disney's world famous characters 'come to life' in the shadow of the enchanting Sleeping Beauty Castle. Snow White, the Seven Dwarfs, Mickey and Minnie Mouse, Goofy, Donald Duck and a multitude of others mingle with the crowds, signing autographs or posing for photographs with spellbound children. Here also is the 147 feet high model of the famous Swiss Matterhorn, an idyllic setting for the highly popular bobsleds and skyway. "Tomorrow's World can be achieved today" prophesied Walt Disney and it was with this object in mind that the futuristic realm of Tomorrowland with its novel form of transport, the People Mover, was constructed. Among some of man's most innovative accomplishments stands Space Mountain, where the intrepid visitor may board a rocket for an "out of this world" space adventure.

Eleven years after the opening of DISNEYLAND, a sixth theme land was added to the original five. New Orleans Square encompasses all the atmosphere and color of the 'Queen City of the Mississippi' in the 1850s: narrow, winding streets, small secluded courtyards, lacy wrought-iron balconies, French and Creole Cafés and elegant shops are crowned by a haunted mansion and the Pirates of the Caribbean. Bear Country was added in 1972. This is a vivid reconstruction of the Great Northwest, highlighted by the Country Bear Jamboree, a performance given by an Audio-Animatronics cast of bears and other wild animals.

Walt Disney's initial $17 million investment is now a $197 million entertainment complex famous throughout the world. Behind the scenes an 'army' of painters, carpenters, electricians, technicians and cleaning crews work diligently to maintain the impeccable appearance of the park...no easy task in a complex which is open seven days a week most of the year. The streets are steam cleaned every day and 20,000 gallons of paint are used every year. A thirty-eight man landscaping staff look after the 500,000 trees, plants and shrubs and at the peak of the summer period 60,000 people are catered for daily: annual consumption of 'fast foods' include 4.5 million hamburgers, 2 million hot dogs, 3 million boxes of popcorn and enough soft drinks to fill a 5

acre lake. Yet, despite the magnitude of the whole enterprise Disney's dreams had not been altogether realized. At the 10th Anniversary celebrations of DISNEYLAND, Walt commented "These past ten years have only been a dress rehearsal. If any of you wants to rest on his laurels, forget it," for Walt Disney was about to embark on his last but many say his greatest dream...WALT DISNEY WORLD.

This time he looked to the eastern U.S.A. and after intensive research, in October 1965 purchased 27,443 acres of pine forest near Orlando in the heart of the sunshine state of Florida. Again the planning began but this time on a far grander scale, which included not only a theme park but also hotels, motels and a wealth of recreational facilities. Sadly, just over a year after the land purchase, Walt Disney died. After working on his last animated film, 'Jungle Book', he was found to be suffering from an advanced state of cancer of the lung and on 15th December 1966 his life ended in St Joseph's Hospital, just across the road from his Burbank Studio.

Fortunately his original ideas for WALT DISNEY WORLD were left in the capable hands of his brother, Roy, and the Disney Organization, who embarked on the creation of a vacation kingdom which would also conserve the natural beauty of the area. In 1967 Legislation was passed by the State of Florida, establishing the Reedy Creek Improvement District and two cities, Bay Lake and Lake Buena Vista. Construction began in 1969 and a two year time limit was set for the completion of Phase I of the project. Over 8,000 workers were involved in this enormous task, which included digging out a 200 acre lake called the Seven Seas Lagoon, developing two championship 18 hole golf courses and constructing 2 luxurious hotels in addition to the six lands of the Magic Kingdom itself. To provide electricity and hot water for heating and cooking systems throughout WALT DISNEY WORLD, a central energy plant was specially built and the 'ingredients' for the park were brought from all points of the compass: huge monorail beams came from Washington State, old

steam locomotives were found by the W.E.D. team in Mexico and restored in Tampa, Florida, jungle cruise boats, steam launches, swanboats and countless other attractions were made up in Tampa and from W.E.D. Enterprises in California came millions of individual pieces to be assembled on the site. As if by magic, these were transformed into even more advanced computer controlled versions of many of DISNEYLAND's favorite attractions. Yet all this was done with a sensitive regard for the requirements of the natural environment: AVAC, a unique trash collection system was installed to maintain the highest level of cleanliness, forty miles of canals were constructed to prevent possible flooding and, in order to avoid depleting local nurseries as DISNEYLAND had done, a Disney Tree Farm, enriched by specially treated effluent provided WALT DISNEY WORLD with all the required trees and plants, at a miraculous rate. Finally 7,500 acres of the actual site were designated as a conservation area and set aside as a wild life sanctuary. The result was what Walt Disney had envisaged, "a showcase to the world for the ingenuity and imagination of American free enterprise."

As opening day drew near the finishing touches were put to shops, restaurants, hotels and campsites and in October 1971 the ceremony took place. Once again the occasion was marked by the presence of the reigning 'superstars' of the entertainment world but tragically this time Walt Disney himself could not witness the event. Instead, it was Roy Disney, the man who had nurtured Walt's dream into reality, who proudly dedicated the park to the memory of his brother: "WALT DISNEY WORLD is a tribute to the philosophy and life of Walter Elias Disney...and to the talents, the dedication, and the loyalty of the entire Disney Organization that made Walt Disney's dream come true. May WALT DISNEY WORLD bring joy and inspiration and new knowledge to all who come to this happy place...a Magic Kingdom where the young at heart of all ages can laugh and play and learn – together."

Captivated by the opportunity to share Walt's beautiful dream 10.8 million people visited WALT DISNEY WORLD in that first year, encouraging the Disney Organization to launch a $200 million expansion program. Gradually the capacity of the theme park has been increased, new attractions added, more accommodation provided and transportation improved. DISNEYLAND...the one that started it all...also continues to grow, for Walt Disney's ability to 'imagineer' for the future has ensured that the stories of DISNEYLAND and WALT DISNEY WORLD will never really have a final chapter. Yet another project originally planned by Disney, has now reached the stages of advanced planning. Phase 2 of WALT DISNEY WORLD, EPCOT, an Experimental Prototype Community of Tomorrow will be a "World Showcase," in which, with all the irresistible magic of Disney, nations will present their history, culture and commerce and the giants of American industry will display the technological advances we can expect to see and enjoy in the world of the future.

Animation *opposite page* transports Disney's audiences into a fantasy world of vivid scenes from 'The Sword in the Stone' *above left,* 'Fantasia' *above and center right,* 'The Jungle Book' *center left,* '101 Dalmatians' *below left,* and 'Robin Hood' *below right.*
Overleaf: The Blue Fairy rescues Pinocchio, but not before he tells her a series of lies, causing his nose to grow longer and longer until it eventually sprouts branches and leaves.

Main Street, U.S.A. in DISNEYLAND *above* recaptures the atmosphere of the 'small home town' and its friendly way of life, as down the street marches the Disneyland Band led by a jubilant Mickey Mouse. It was Mickey who assisted Roy Disney at the opening ceremony of WALT DISNEY WORLD *below* and Disney's much loved characters still contribute greatly to the joy of these magical realms: a little girl *left* watches intently as Minnie Mouse cuddles her friend; a young fan *right* looks admiringly at Minnie and children *overleaf* delight in a memorable meeting with Minnie, Mickey and Goofy.

Walt Disney's aspiration to create a world in which the young at heart of all ages could laugh and play together has been fulfilled... for here, while children frolic with Donald Duck and Robin Hood *above and below,* or enjoy a moment of real tenderness with Goofy *left,* an adult visitor *right* shares a joke with Tigger. As night falls in WALT DISNEY WORLD *overleaf,* passengers board the 'Admiral Joe Fowler' at the Liberty Square Riverboat Landing.

Fantasyland is the land where dreams come true, where children can wander hand in hand with their favorite Disney characters *above*, and where at night the magic castle of DISNEYLAND *left*, lit by a blaze of fireworks assumes all the qualities of a fairy-tale. Here too, the classic stories of childhood like that of Snow White and the Seven Dwarfs *below* become 'reality'.

WALT DISNEY WORLD's magic palace-fortress, Cinderella Castle *right* rises dramatically at the end of Main Street. Rainbow-colored balloons *overleaf* shimmer against the unbroken blue of a cloudless sky.

An encounter with Mickey Mouse *above* or Donald Duck *right* is a particularly special moment for a child, but Disney's world awakens the child in people of all ages as they soar above Fantasyland aboard Dumbo the elephant *above right and below* or on the lofty Skyway *left*, or enter the Whale's jaws *top*, explore Tom Sawyer Island *above left* or delve into the mysteries of Tomorrowland *below right*.

High above the Magic Kingdom *overleaf*, fireworks shower Cinderella Castle with multicolored light.

No matter whether like Pluto *left* and Donald Duck *right*, Disney's characters are of his own creation, or whether like Pooh Bear *below* they are 'adopted' from the works of others, they all possess, like Dopey *above*, that lovable quality which evokes in children a uniquely warm response.

Overleaf: In the light of the setting sun, the Empress Lilly Riverboat finds its reflection in the still waters of Lake Buena Vista.

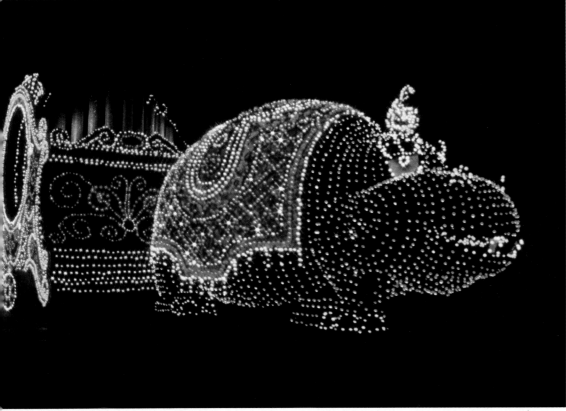

Night-time in DISNEYLAND, and WALT DISNEY WORLD casts its own distinctive spell when brilliantly colored lights bring to life a vivid range of characters and scenes in the Electrical Parade on Main Street *above, center and below left,* and floodlighting adds to the majesty of Cinderella Castle *below.*

Even 'It's a small world' *overleaf,* a three-dimensional world inhabited by 500 Audio – Animatronics children and animals, assumes a special atmosphere under its night-time illuminations *above and top.*

Glowing red against a darkened sky *above right,* the Sunshine Pavilion in Adventureland provides a delightful Polynesian show in which, with the aid of Audio-Animatronics, birds sing and Tiki gods and goddesses chant in a fantasy recalling legends of the South Seas.

Disneyland Trains from Main Street Station carry passengers to a daunting display of giant reptiles in the Primeval World of the Dinosaurs *below right.*

At the heart of DISNEYLAND's Fantasyland rises Sleeping Beauty Castle *above left* while in WALT DISNEY WORLD's Fantasyland *below left* Captain Nemo's Nautilus provides a glimpse of the ocean's depths, 20,000 Leagues Under the Sea.

Tomorrowland with its rocket rides *below* and its submarine voyages *above* and *center left* offers a preview of some of the fascinating developments of the future.

WALT DISNEY WORLD's golf courses *right* present a picturesque challenge to golfing enthusiasts.

Transport is all part of the fun...ranging from the vessels of a fictional past like Captain Hook's galleon *far left* or the Mark Twain Steamboat *bottom* to the submarine *above* which glides silently through a South Sea coral lagoon and the streamlined monorail *overleaf* which demonstrates a transport system of tomorrow. The company too is unusual, for mingling with the crowd are characters like the Little Pigs *left and below* and Mickey Mouse *below left*. The pictures *overleaf* provide a glimpse of the infinite excitement and variety of DISNEYLAND.

The Mark Twain Steamboat passing through Frontierland *above*, the monorail glinting in the sunlight at the foot of the Matterhorn *left*, a horse waiting patiently outside Sleeping Beauty castle *below*, and the colorful spectacle of a group of Fire Department musicians *above right* or of Fantasyland's attractions *right* ...all serve to demonstrate the infinite variety of a world in which everything seems possible.

On the banks of the Rivers of America, Frontierland and Liberty Square reflect America's pride in a history shaped by the vision of its early pioneers. The Columbia *left and above* passes silently by as an Indian watches closely from the undergrowth and a log raft *below* crosses to Tom Sawyer Island *bottom* and *below right*. The Olde Worlde Antique Shop *above right* recalls the eve of independence, 1776 and the gardens of the Polynesian Village Resort Hotel capture the exoticism of the South Seas.

Overleaf: Captain Hook's Pirate Ship waits at its moorings in Fantasyland.

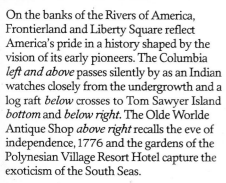

A vintage truck *below* advertises the Carnation Ice Cream Parlor.

To take a ride on a horse-drawn street-car *above* or aboard a brightly painted steam train *below right* is to step into a world inhabited by Alice, the Walrus and the White Rabbit *left*, by Mickey and Minnie Mouse *below left*, Pinocchio *right*, Donald Duck *bottom* and by numerous other famous personalities.

From Steam Age to Space Age *overleaf*, inside Space Mountain the 'stout at heart' board rockets for an exciting adventure in Tomorrowland.

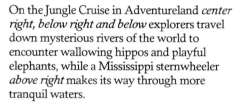

On the Jungle Cruise in Adventureland *center right, below right and below* explorers travel down mysterious rivers of the world to encounter wallowing hippos and playful elephants, while a Mississippi sternwheeler *above right* makes its way through more tranquil waters.

Skull Rock Cove *top,* is aptly sited near Captain Hook's Galley in Fantasyland and the colorful parade *left* is one of many held in Liberty Square.

Mickey Mouse *above* obligingly holds the pin for a keen golfer while the steam train *left* passes round the perimeter of the Magic Kingdom.

Overleaf: Crystal chandeliers, domed skylights and indoor trees and plants recall the elegance of the Victorian Age in the Crystal Palace Restaurant.

The buildings on Main Street, WALT
DISNEY WORLD *above and left* form an
impressive backdrop for the many colorful
parades and processions which pass by, and
together with the imposing City Hall on Town
Square *below* and Cinderella Castle *right,* they
provide striking examples of the
'imagineering' and the construction skill of the
W.E.D. team.

Beneath the fairy-tale towers of Cinderella Castle *left*, Alice strolls arm in arm with the White Rabbit and the Walrus, and Mickey Mouse *above and right* entertains admiring onlookers while an encounter with more Disney characters *below* provides the ideal opportunity to pose for the camera.

As night falls *overleaf* a new kind of magic and excitement takes over when Cinderella Castle and Main Street glitter with a thousand lights.

Designed to give the visitor the feeling of having lived, if only briefly, during America's pioneer days, Davy Crockett Explorer Canoes *above left* provide an appropriate means of travelling through Frontierland.

Watched through larger than life glasses *left*, Mickey *above* and Tigger *below, below left* and *right* befriend young admirers.

DISNEYLAND and WALT DISNEY
WORLD are ablaze with color...from the
natural rich greens of the lush vegetation on
the banks of the Rivers of America *right* to the
flowers which adorn the Topiary gardens of
'It's a Small World' *below left* or the shops on
Main Street *below right,* and the brilliant
displays of Mickey Mouse balloons *above left.*

Set against this colorful background a horse-
drawn trolley on Main Street *above right* and
two jazz musicians in New Orleans Square
below echo a bygone era.

From the prancing steeds of King Arthur's
Carousel in Fantasyland a little girl waves
coyly *above* and two more children *overleaf*
journey bright-eyed to a land which is
uniquely theirs.

DISNEYLAND and WALT DISNEY
WORLD are ablaze with color...from the
natural rich greens of the lush vegetation on
the banks of the Rivers of America *right* to the
flowers which adorn the Topiary gardens of
'It's a Small World' *below left* or the shops on
Main Street *below right,* and the brilliant
displays of Mickey Mouse balloons *above left.*

Set against this colorful background a horse-
drawn trolley on Main Street *above right* and
two jazz musicians in New Orleans Square
below echo a bygone era.

From the prancing steeds of King Arthur's
Carousel in Fantasyland a little girl waves
coyly *above* and two more children *overleaf*
journey bright-eyed to a land which is
uniquely theirs.

In Tomorrowland, the DISNEYLAND People Mover System *above left* provides a noiseless, smooth preview of city mass transportation and rocket ships *left, below and overleaf* blast off to leave this earth for the world of tomorrow.

Towering high above DISNEYLAND's Fantasyland is Matterhorn Mountain *above and top*, an exact scale replica of the famous Swiss peak, while far below gigantic cups and saucers *right* recall the Mad Tea Party.

At the crack of Timothy Mouse's whip Dumbo Flying Elephants *below left* soar over Fantasyland in DISNEYLAND.

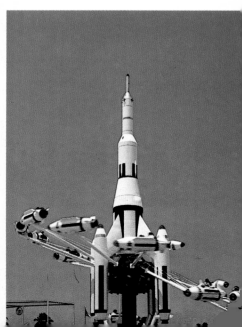

om the moment when visitors have their
t meeting with Mickey Mouse *above right*
with Brer Fox *right* to the moment when
ht-time illuminations flood Sleeping
auty Castle *above left*, the atmosphere is
e of fun of all kinds *above and below* and of
spitality. It is highly appropriate therefore
t the building in WALT DISNEY WORLD
ow left should be known as Hospitality
use.

Nightfall brings a change of atmosphere and pace as the crowds retire from the attractions of the streets *above left* to the indoor entertainment of the Golden Horseshoe *left and below left* or watch the antics of the Audio-Animatronics bears *above*. The setting sun lengthens the shadows of the boats on the Rivers of America *below* and darkness brings additional mystique to the Haunted Mansion *above right* and a special beauty to Lake Buena Vista *right*.

Overleaf: Mickey Mouse tees off on the 12th hole of a championship golf course.

The Admiral Joe Fowler draws steadily away from Tom Sawyer Island *above left*.

At night this is a dazzling world of sights, sounds and lights which accentuate the Grand Victorian outline of the Crystal Palace Restaurant *above* or gleam mysteriously from the rigging of Captain Hook's pirate vessel *below left*. In the Polynesian Village Resort Hotel *below* a dancer performs in traditional dress and at Fort Wilderness Campground *right* a camp-fire provides the focal point for a sing-along.

Gulf Hospitality House, WALT DISNEY
~~WO~~RLD *above,* 'The Walt Disney Story'
~~disp~~lays memorabilia and filmed highlights of
~~the~~ master showman's life, recounted in his
~~ow~~n words and including the birth of
~~char~~acters such as Mickey Mouse and Donald
~~Duc~~k *left.*

~~A b~~rightly painted fire engine *right* provides
~~a m~~eans of taking a nostalgic trip down Main
~~Stre~~et and the Richard F. Irvine in Frontierland
~~belo~~w recalls Mark Twain's days of the
~~Mis~~sissippi sternwheelers.

In Main Street immaculately costumed bands
march in perfect time *center left* and give
concerts *above left* to audiences that may well
include characters like Pinocchio *above*,
Mickey Mouse *below left* and Pooh Bear
bottom carrying his inevitable pot of 'hunny'.

Also in Main Street passengers board a
horseless carriage *below* while on Discovery
Island *above right* a parrot greets a privileged
visitor with its outstretched, brilliantly colored
wings.

Sunlight shimmers on the waters that
punctuate a Walt Disney golf course *below
right*.

A cluster of balloons *overleaf* adds brilliance to
the delicate spires of Cinderella Castle.

WALT DISNEY WORLD's Contemporary Resort *above* is one of the world's most dynamic new hotels. Here monorails *below* glide noiselessly through the open nine-story Grand Canyon Concourse *above left* where guests may dine and shop and admire the 90 foot mural which gives the Concourse its name. The resort also offers a wide variety of recreation activities on its beach *right* or in the pool area *below left*. Though less futuristic in design the pool *center left* at River Country is also very attractive.

Overleaf: The Polynesian Village Resort Hotel nestles among the lush vegetation of this tropical 'island of enchantment'.

DISNEYLAND and WALT DISNEY
WORLD offer a new kind of vacation
experience with all the luxurious
accommodation of modern futuristic design
below left and all the romantic atmosphere of
the illuminated recapturings of a vivid and
eventful past *above right and left.*

Sailing *above* and golf *below* are but two of
the endless attractions that also include the
challenging Grand Prix raceway *right* and the
exhilarating 260 foot water slide *below right*
…and all this is crowned by the presence of
Disney's charming characters *bottom.*

Disney's 'theme' parks deal in everything from nostalgia to space technology, their transportation systems represent a wide variety of types and eras and their attractions are seemingly endless.

Parades *left*, reconstructions from the past *above left*, flying elephants *above*, colorful displays of flowers *below*, fairy-tale castles *below left* and the heroes of Disney's most popular films *above and below right*…all serve to make a visit to DISNEYLAND or WALT DISNEY WORLD an unforgettable experience in what Disney himself intended to be a 'truly happy place'.

WINDWARD
An imprint owned by W. H. Smith & Son Ltd., Reg'd no. 237811 England,
trading as W.H.S. Distributors, Freemens Common, Aylestone Road, Leicester
© 1979. Walt Disney Production
Display and text filmsetting by Focus Photoset, London, England.
Colour separations by Fercrom, Barcelona, Spain.
Printed and bound by SAGDOS-Brugherio (MI), Italy.
ISBN 0-7112-0017-3